DOVER · THRIFT · EDITIONS

First Fig
and Other Poems

EDNA ST. VINCENT MILLAY

DOVER PUBLICATIONS, INC.
Mineola, New York

DOVER THRIFT EDITIONS

GENERAL EDITOR: PAUL NEGRI

EDITOR OF THIS VOLUME: JOSLYN T. PINE

Bibliographical Note

This Dover edition, first published in 2000, is an unabridged republication of the following two volumes: *A Few Figs from Thistles: Poems and Sonnets*, originally published by Harper & Brothers Publishers, New York, 1922; and *Second April*, originally published by Harper & Brothers Publishers, New York, 1921. A new introductory Note has been specially prepared for this edition.

Library of Congress Cataloging-in-Publication Data

Millay, Edna St. Vincent, 1892–1950.
    First fig and other poems / Edna St. Vincent Millay.
       p. cm. — (Dover thrift editions)
    ISBN 0-486-41104-4 (pbk.)
     I. Title. II. Series.

PS3525.I495 A6 2000
811'.52—dc21

                                99-053136

Manufactured in the United States of America
Dover Publications, Inc., 31 East 2nd Street, Mineola, N.Y. 11501

Note

*. . . an exile far out upon the world's forsaken rim,
her wild feet forever seeking Beauty.*

(Edna St. Vincent Millay as described by fellow poet
and lifelong friend, Arthur Davison Ficke)

EDNA ST. VINCENT MILLAY (1892–1950), poet, playwright, feminist and humanist ranks among the greats in American poetry, despite the fact that her reputation during the last half of the century has been mostly in decline. Whatever current fashion literary circles mandate, most serious critics from her time and beyond generally agree that she is America's best practitioner of the sonnet form; and at the height of her fame and popularity, she was considered America's finest living lyric poet. While the American literati could be fickle in their evaluations of her poetry, at least two of her British contemporaries were unequivocal in their admiration for her work: her idol, A. E. Housman, and Thomas Hardy, who stated that the two great contributions America made to the twenties were its architectural innovations and Edna St. Vincent Millay.

A native of the Maine seacoast, and the eldest of three sisters, Millay was nurtured in the arts by a doting mother,[1] Cora Buzzelle Millay, who schooled her precocious daughter in the traditional forms of poetry. In fact, it was remarked by one of Millay's lifelong friends, Floyd Dell—a fellow Provincetown Player from her Greenwich Village days—that "her mother put more emphasis on her respecting the conventions of art than the conventions of behavior." Telling words, especially considering that not only would Millay come to epitomize the free-spirited woman of the twenties, but also because her critics would later devalue her poetry for bypassing the modernist bandwagon.

---

[1]The bond between mother and daughter was especially strong because Millay's father—Henry Tolman Millay, a compulsive gambler who squandered his family's meager resources—was sent away by his wife when the child was only seven.

Instead, Millay adhered unwaveringly to conventional forms through-
out her distinguished career as a poet. She composed her first poem at
the age of five; it consisted of three rhymed couplets on the theme of
"One Bird." Her first published poem, "Forest Trees," appeared in *St.
Nicholas* magazine when Millay was only fourteen. This extraordinary
magazine for children, an inspiration to many budding American poets
and writers, would later publish several more of her poems, one of
which would be anthologized in the volume *Current Literature* and
start "E. Vincent Millay," as she then signed her work, on the path to
wide acclaim.

The year 1912 was a fateful one for the arts in America, ushering in
the experimental movements that would come to dominate the century,
fueled by the revolution in thought inspired by Charles Darwin, Karl
Marx, and especially Sigmund Freud. It was also a fateful year for the
twenty-year-old Millay who entered the poetry contest sponsored by an
anthology called *The Lyric Year*[2] which sought to publish the 100 best
American poems written during 1912. The judges awarded prizes to the
top three poems only; so when her poem "Renascence"—considered by
many to be the best in the volume—took fourth place and received no
prize at all, there was a huge storm of protest. As one critic observed,
"The young girl from Camden, Maine, became famous through *not* re-
ceiving the prize." What made the controversy all the more surprising
was the fact that "Renascence" garnered a fervent following despite its
conventional form, and without even a nod to modernism.

At a reading of "Renascence" at Whitehall Inn in Camden, Maine,
the poet caught the attention of Miss Catherine B. Dow, head of the
National Training School of the YWCA, and inspired the influential
woman to become her patroness—raising money and arranging for
Millay to attend Vassar College. Finally, the poem also won her the
high esteem and lasting friendship of two poets who were both to be-
come key figures in her personal and professional life—Witter
Bynner and Arthur Davison Ficke. In fact, Ficke would grow gradu-
ally in importance to become her mentor, and is thought by some
scholars to have been the great love of Millay's life, despite their mar-
riage to others.

---

[2]Published by Mitchell Kennerly, later the publisher of her first volume of poetry
Renascence and Other Poems (1917) and her third, *Second April* (1921). This proved to
be an ill-starred association for Millay, who suffered through numerous postponements
and received scant remuneration from Kennerly throughout their relationship. In 1923,
Harper & Brothers became Millay's permanent publishers and soon after reissued the
two volumes published by Kennerly, as well as *A Few Figs from Thistles*, originally pub-
lished in chapbook form in 1920 by Frank Shay, owner of a Village bookshop, because
of Mitchell Kennerly's endless delays.

At Vassar, Millay enjoyed significant celebrity not only as a literary light, but also for her work in theatre where, it is generally believed, she began having intimate relationships with women. In addition to her acting and poetry, she gained an awareness of social issues like the suffragist movement and women's rights. It was in the course of a series of lectures on the subject that Millay met Inez Milholland, one of the most stirring of the speakers. She was a prominent Vassar alumna of 1909, known as the "Amazon Beauty" of the suffragist movement, a glamorous and inspiring figure to many impressionable young women like Millay. Milholland's tragic premature death would occur about a year later—in 1916—leaving her husband, Eugen Jan Boissevain, a grieving widower. His path would intertwine fatefully with Millay's a few years later.

In 1917, the year of her graduation from Vassar, she published her first book, *Renascence and Other Poems*. She also moved to Greenwich Village in New York City where she dwelt in a 9-foot-wide attic, leading a rather bohemian and "poor but merry" life among fellow writers and intellectuals. Here she devoted herself to writing poetry and prose pieces to bolster her perpetually scant finances, publishing the latter in various magazines under the pseudonym "Nancy Boyd" to keep her poetry pure from the taint of her "hack work," as it was called by some. She also joined the Provincetown Players for whom she acted as well as wrote verse plays, her first—in 1919—being *Aria da Capo*, an anti-war piece. It enjoyed considerable success in New York, as well as with little theater and college groups all over the country, and a French version was staged in Paris. Her circle continually widened, encompassing—among many others—George Cram ("Jig") Cook and Susan Glaspell (co-founders of the Provincetown Players), Emma Goldman, Eugene O'Neill, John Reed, Max Eastman, Djuna Barnes, Charles and Albert Boni (whose Washington Square Bookshop was a meeting place for the local little theatre movement) and Floyd Dell—who later proposed marriage. Millay, a self-proclaimed bisexual, refused, intent as she was on preserving her freedom.

In 1920, *A Few Figs from Thistles* was published and became an enormous success. Millay was hailed variously as "the poet laureate of the twenties," "the spokesman for the new woman," and "the voice of rebellious, flaming youth." Many of the poems seemed to advocate the same kind of sexual freedom for women that men already enjoyed. But the volume's popularity cut like a two-edged sword for Millay since it created a somewhat frivolous impression of an essentially serious artist. The timing of its publication was also seen by some of her defenders as unfortunate, coming as it did before *Second April*, which was published in 1921. *Second April* was greeted with far more critical acclaim by the literary community, who regarded it and the volumes that followed as more stable and mature than *A Few Figs from Thistles*, rather than merely a resumption of the mood and concerns of her first volume of poetry, *Renascence and Other Poems*. This circumstance, along with her feminist leanings and involvement in other social causes (e.g., the Sacco and Vanzetti affair), paved the way for a later critical backlash that included such major literary figures as Cleanth Brooks, John Crowe Ransom, and John Ciardi, who covertly attacked Millay's politics and gender through the approach of her art. In smaller measure, as mentioned before, her progressive decline was also attributable to the emergence of a new group of poets—T. S. Eliot, Ezra Pound, Wallace Stevens, and Marianne Moore, among others—who were considered more fresh and innovative in their contribution to the genre of poetry than Millay.

Thanks to indefatigable hard work, the poet could finally afford to bring her beloved mother and sisters to the Village to live with her. Their residence at 25 Charlton Street was the site of many memorable literary soirées, where Millay began to collect a long string of admirers, notable among them Edmund Wilson, then an assistant editor at *Vanity Fair* who courted her by inviting her contributions to the magazine. It was at least partly due to Wilson's instigation that in 1921 Millay went on a two-year sojourn to Europe as a foreign correspondent for *Vanity Fair*, at about the same time she was finding her Village life arid and fatiguing. In Paris, she became acquainted with members of the so-called "lost generation" (a common and incorrect translation of Gertrude Stein's original phrase, "la génération *du temps* perdu") like F. Scott and Zelda Fitzgerald, with whom she was singularly unimpressed. Others who came within her sphere while she was abroad were Stephen Vincent and William Rose Benét, Edgar Lee Masters, Dorothy Thompson, and the composer Deems Taylor. While the experience broadened her horizons and her list of acquaintances, she was by turns homesick and depressed by the post-war gloom in some of the places she visited, and first suffered the intestinal problems that were to plague her for years to come. When she finally returned to the States on the verge of thirty, she was severely physically ill and without any marital prospects; all her lovers had abandoned the idea of marriage to her, and poetry remained her grand passion.

While 1922 may have marked a low point in her physical and emotional life, the year marked a peak in her professional life. Millay was awarded the Pulitzer Prize for "The Ballad of the Harp-Weaver" (a new poem published in booklet form by Frank Shay), an expanded edition of *A Few Figs*, and for eight sonnets included in the *American Miscellany of Poetry*, making her the first woman poet to receive this prestigious award. It was also in the same year that—through mutual friends—she had her third and most fateful encounter with Eugen Boissevain, the Dutch businessman who was the widower of Inez Milholland, whom Millay had met at Vassar. This time the two fell in love, and married in 1923. Boissevain was a man of the world, something of a *bon vivant*, and at the same time possessed of a sensitive spirit. He was twelve years older than Millay, and took the role of protector in the poet's life, shielding her from all responsibilities save writing. A paternal figure—perhaps the first in her life—he not only provided a nurturing environment but also acted as her business manager, arranging all of her readings and public appearances. Under her husband's influence, Millay wrote prolifically and her career thrived for a time.

In 1925, after briefly residing in the Village together, the couple took up permanent residence at Steepletop, their 700-acre berry farm situated in the Berkshire foothills in Austerlitz, New York, where they gradually renovated the house and reclaimed the farmland over a period of years. Here they lived together harmoniously and like "two bachelors," since theirs was rumored to be an open marriage. Steepletop would become their primary residence for the next twenty-five years—the rest of their lives, as it would turn out.

Contents

Contents

First Fig

and Other Poems

First Fig

My candle burns at both ends;
    It will not last the night;
But ah, my foes, and oh, my friends—
    It gives a lovely light!

Second Fig

Safe upon the solid rock the ugly houses stand:
Come and see my shining palace built upon the sand!

Recuerdo

We were very tired, we were very merry—
We had gone back and forth all night on the ferry.
It was bare and bright, and smelled like a stable—
But we looked into a fire, we leaned across a table,
We lay on the hill-top underneath the moon;
And the whistles kept blowing, and the dawn came soon.

We were very tired, we were very merry—
We had gone back and forth all night on the ferry;
And you ate an apple, and I ate a pear,
From a drozen of each we had bought somewhere;
And the sky went wan, and the wind came cold,
And the sun rose dripping, a bucketful of gold.

We were very tired, we were very merry,
We had gone back and forth all night on the ferry.
We hailed, "Good morrow, mother!" to a shawl-covered head,
And bought a morning paper, which neither of us read;
And she wept, "God bless you!" for the apples and the pears,
And we gave her all our money but our subway fares.

1

Thursday

And if I loved you Wednesday,
    Well, what is that to you?
I do not love you Thursday—
    So much is true.

And why you come complaining
    Is more than I can see.
I loved you Wednesday,—yes—but what
    Is that to me?

To the Not Impossible Him

How shall I know, unless I go
    To Cairo and Cathay,
Whether or not this blessed spot
    Is blest in every way?

Now it may be, the flower for me
    Is this beneath my nose;
How shall I tell, unless I smell
    The Carthaginian rose?

The fabric of my faithful love
    No power shall dim or ravel
Whilst I stay here,—but oh, my dear,
    If I should ever travel!

MacDougal Street

As I went walking up and down to take the evening air,
    (Sweet to meet upon the street, why must I be so shy?)
I saw him lay his hand upon her torn black hair;
    ("Little dirty Latin child, let the lady by!")

The women squatting on the stoops were slovenly and fat,
    (Lay me out in organdie, lay me out in lawn!)
And everywhere I stepped there was a baby or a cat;
    (Lord, God in Heaven, will it never be dawn?)

The fruit-carts and clam-carts were ribald as a fair,
    (Pink nets and wet shells trodden under heel)

She had haggled from the fruit-man of his rotting ware;
  (I shall never get to sleep, the way I feel!)

He walked like a king through the filth and the clutter,
  (Sweet to meet upon the street, why did you glance me by?)
But he caught the quaint Italian quip she flung him from the gutter;
  (What can there be to cry about that I should lie and cry?)

He laid his darling hand upon her little black head,
  (I wish I were a ragged child with ear-rings in my ears!)
And he said she was a baggage to have said what she had said;
  (Truly I shall be ill unless I stop these tears!)

The Singing-Woman from the Wood's Edge

What should I be but a prophet and a liar,
Whose mother was a leprechaun, whose father was a friar?
Teethed on a crucifix and cradled under water,
What should I be but the fiend's god-daughter?

And who should be my playmates but the adder and the frog,
That was got beneath a furze-bush and born in a bog?
And what should be my singing, that was christened at an altar,
But Aves and Credos and Psalms out of the Psalter?

You will see such webs on the wet grass, maybe,
As a pixie-mother weaves for her baby,
You will find such flame at the wave's weedy ebb
As flashes in the meshes of a mer-mother's web,

But there comes to birth no common spawn
From the love of a priest for a leprechaun,
And you never have seen and you never will see
Such things as the things that swaddled me!

After all's said and after all's done,
What should I be but a harlot and a nun?

In through the bushes, on any foggy day,
My Da would come a-swishing of the drops away,
With a prayer for my death and a groan for my birth,
A-mumbling of his beads for all that he was worth.

And there sit my Ma, her knees beneath her chin,
A-looking in his face and a-drinking of it in,
And a-marking in the moss some funny little saying
That would mean just the opposite of all that he was praying!

He taught me the holy-talk of Vesper and of Matin,
He heard me my Greek and he heard me my Latin,
He blessed me and crossed me to keep my soul from evil,
And we watched him out of sight, and we conjured up the devil!

Oh, the things I haven't seen and the things I haven't known,
What with hedges and ditches till after I was grown,
And yanked both ways by my mother and my father,
With a "Which would you better?" and a "Which would you rather?"

With him for a sire and her for a dam,
What should I be but just what I am?

She Is Overheard Singing

Oh, Prue she has a patient man,
    And Joan a gentle lover,
And Agatha's Arth' is a hug-the-hearth,—
    But my true love's a rover!

Mig, her man's as good as cheese
    And honest as a briar,
Sue tells her love what he's thinking of,—
    But my dear lad's a liar!

Oh, Sue and Prue and Agatha!
    Are thick with Mig and Joan!
They bite their threads and shake their heads
    And gnaw my name like a bone;

And Prue says, "Mine's a patient man,
    As never snaps me up,"
And Agatha, "Arth' is a hug-the-hearth,
    Could live content in a cup,"

Sue's man's mind is like good jell—
    All one color, and clear—
And Mig's no call to think at all
    What's to come next year,

While Joan makes boast of a gentle lad,
    That's troubled with that and this;—
But they all would give the life they live
    For a look from the man I kiss!

Cold he slants his eyes about,
    And few enough's his choice,—

Though he'd slip me clean for a nun, or a queen,
  Or a beggar with knots in her voice,—

And Agatha will turn awake
  When her good man sleeps sound,
And Mig and Sue and Joan and Prue
  Will hear the clock strike round,

For Prue she has a patient man,
  As asks not when or why,
And Mig and Sue have naught to do
  But peep who's passing by,

Joan is paired with a putterer
  That bastes and tastes and salts,
And Agatha's Arth' is a hug-the-hearth,—
  But my true love is false!

The Prisoner

    All right,
    Go ahead!
    What's in a name?
    I guess I'll be locked into
    As much as I'm locked out of!

The Unexplorer

  There was a road ran past our house
  Too lovely to explore.
  I asked my mother once—she said
  That if you followed where it led
  It brought you to the milk-man's door.
  (That's why I have not traveled more.)

Grown-up

Was it for this I uttered prayers,
  And sobbed and cursed and kicked the stairs,
  That now, domestic as a plate,
  I should retire at half-past eight?

The Penitent

I had a little Sorrow,
   Born of a little Sin,
I found a room all damp with gloom
   And shut us all within;
And, "Little Sorrow, weep," said I,
"And, Little Sin, pray God to die,
And I upon the floor will lie
   And think how bad I've been!"

Alas for pious planning—
   It mattered not a whit!
As far as gloom went in that room,
   The lamp might have been lit!
My Little Sorrow would not weep,
My Little Sin would go to sleep—
To save my soul I could not keep
   My graceless mind on it!

So up I got in anger,
   And took a book I had,
And put a ribbon on my hair
   To please a passing lad.
And, "One thing there's no getting by—
I've been a wicked girl," said I;
"But if I can't be sorry, why,
   I might as well be glad!"

Daphne

Why do you follow me?—
Any moment I can be
Nothing but a laurel-tree.

Any moment of the chase
I can leave you in my place
A pink bough for your embrace.

Yet if over hill and hollow
Still it is your will to follow,
I am off;—to heel, Apollo!

Portrait by a Neighbor

Before she has her floor swept
 Or her dishes done,
Any day you'll find her
 A-sunning in the sun!

It's long after midnight
 Her key's in the lock,
And you never see her chimney smoke
 Till past ten o'clock!

She digs in her garden
 With a shovel and a spoon,
She weeds her lazy lettuce
 By the light of the moon.

She walks up the walk
 Like a woman in a dream,
She forgets she borrowed butter
 And pays you back cream!

Her lawn looks like a meadow,
 And if she mows the place
She leaves the clover standing
 And the Queen Anne's lace!

Midnight Oil

Cut if you will, with Sleep's dull knife,
Each day to half its length, my friend,—
The years that Time takes off *my* life,
 He'll take from off the other end!

The Merry Maid

Oh, I am grown so free from care
 Since my heart broke!
I set my throat against the air,
 I laugh at simple folk!

There's little kind and little fair
 Is worth its weight in smoke

To me, that's grown so free from care
　　Since my heart broke!

Lass, if to sleep you would repair
　　As peaceful as you woke,
Best not besiege your lover there
　　For just the words he spoke
To me, that's grown so free from care
　　Since my heart broke!

To Kathleen

Still must the poet as of old,
In barren attic bleak and cold,
Starve, freeze, and fashion verses to
Such things as flowers and song and you;

Still as of old his being give
In Beauty's name, while she may live,
Beauty that may not die as long
As there are flowers and you and song.

To S. M.

IF HE SHOULD LIE A-DYING

I am not willing you should go
Into the earth, where Helen went;
She is awake by now, I know.
Where Cleopatra's anklets rust
You will not lie with my consent;
And Sappho is a roving dust;
Cressid could love again; Dido,
Rotted in state, is restless still;
You leave me much against my will.

The Philosopher

And what are you that, missing you,
　　I should be kept awake
As many nights as there are days
　　With weeping for your sake?

And what are you that, missing you,
    As many days as crawl
I should be listening to the wind
    And looking at the wall?

I know a man that's a braver man
    And twenty men as kind,
And what are you, that you should be
    The one man in my mind?

Yet women's ways are witless ways,
    As any sage will tell,—
And what am I, that I should love
    So wisely and so well?

FOUR SONNETS

I

Love, though for this you riddle me with darts,
And drag me at your chariot till I die,—
Oh, heavy prince! Oh, panderer of hearts!—
Yet hear me tell how in their throats they lie
Who shout you mighty: thick about my hair,
Day in, day out, your ominous arrows purr,
Who still am free, unto no querulous care
A fool, and in no temple worshiper!
I, that have bared me to your quiver's fire,
Lifted my face into its puny rain,
Do wreathe you Impotent to Evoke Desire
As you are Powerless to Elicit Pain!
(Now will the god, for blasphemy so brave,
Punish me, surely, with the shaft I crave!)

II

I think I should have loved you presently,
And given in earnest words I flung in jest;
And lifted honest eyes for you to see,
And caught your hand against my cheek and breast;
And all my pretty follies flung aside

That won you to me, and beneath your gaze,
Naked of reticence and shorn of pride,
Spread like a chart my little wicked ways.
I, that had been to you, had you remained,
But one more waking from a recurrent dream,
Cherish no less the certain stakes I gained,
And walk your memory's halls, austere, supreme,
A ghost in marble of a girl you knew
Who would have loved you in a day or two.

III

Oh, think not I am faithful to a vow!
Faithless am I save to love's self alone.
Were you not lovely I would leave you now:
After the feet of beauty fly my own.
Were you not still my hunger's rarest food,
And water ever to my wildest thirst,
I would desert you—think not but I would!—
And seek another as I sought you first.
But you are mobile as the veering air,
And all your charms more changeful than the tide,
Wherefore to be inconstant is no care:
I have but to continue at your side.
So wanton, light and false, my love, are you,
I am most faithless when I most am true.

IV

I shall forget you presently, my dear,
So make the most of this, your little day,
Your little month, your little half a year,
Ere I forget, or die, or move away,
And we are done forever; by and by
I shall forget you, as I said, but now,
If you entreat me with your loveliest lie
I will protest you with my favorite vow.
I would indeed that love were longer-lived,
And vows were not so brittle as they are,
But so it is, and nature has contrived

To struggle on without a break thus far,—
Whether or not we find what we are seeking
Is idle, biologically speaking.

Spring

To what purpose, April, do you return again?
Beauty is not enough.
You can no longer quiet me with the redness
Of little leaves opening stickily.
I know what I know.
The sun is hot on my neck as I observe
The spikes of the crocus.
The smell of the earth is good.
It is apparent that there is no death.
But what does that signify?
Not only under ground are the brains of men
Eaten by maggots.
Life in itself
Is nothing,
An empty cup, a flight of uncarpeted stairs.
It is not enough that yearly, down this hill,
April
Comes like an idiot, babbling and strewing flowers.

City Trees

The trees along this city street,
   Save for the traffic and the trains,
Would make a sound as thin and sweet
   As trees in country lanes.

And people standing in their shade
   Out of a shower, undoubtedly
Would hear such music as is made
   Upon a country tree.

Oh, little leaves that are so dumb
   Against the shrieking city air,
I watch you when the wind has come,—
   I know what sound is there.

The Blue-Flag in the Bog

God had called us, and we came;
   Our loved Earth to ashes left;
Heaven was a neighbor's house,
   Open flung to us, bereft.

Gay the lights of Heaven showed,
   And 'twas God who walked ahead;
Yet I wept along the road,
   Wanting my own house instead.

Wept unseen, unheeded cried,
   "All you things my eyes have kissed,
Fare you well! We meet no more,
   Lovely, lovely tattered mist!

Weary wings that rise and fall
   All day long above the fire!"—
Red with heat was every wall,
   Rough with heat was every wire—

"Fare you well, you little winds
   That the flying embers chase!
Fare you well, you shuddering day,
   With your hands before your face!

And, ah, blackened by strange blight,
   Or to a false sun unfurled,
Now forevermore goodbye,
   All the gardens in the world!

On the windless hills of Heaven,
   That I have no wish to see,
White, eternal lilies stand,
   By a lake of ebony.

But the Earth forevermore
   Is a place where nothing grows,—
Dawn will come, and no bud break;
   Evening, and no blossom close.

Spring will come, and wander slow
   Over an indifferent land,
Stand beside an empty creek,
   Hold a dead seed in her hand."

God had called us, and we came,
    But the blessed road I trod
Was a bitter road to me,
    And at heart I questioned God.

"Though in Heaven," I said, "be all
    That the heart would most desire,
Held Earth naught save souls of sinners
    Worth the saving from a fire?

Withered grass,—the wasted growing!
    Aimless ache of laden boughs!"
Little things God had forgotten
    Called me, from my burning house

"Though in Heaven," I said, "be all
    That the eye could ask to see,
All the things I ever knew
    Are this blaze in back of me."

"Though in Heaven," I said, "be all
    That the ear could think to lack,
All the things I ever knew
    Are this roaring at my back."

It was God who walked ahead,
    Like a shepherd to the fold;
In his footsteps fared the weak,
    And the weary and the old,

Glad enough of gladness over,
    Ready for the peace to be,—
But a thing God had forgotten
    Was the growing bones of me.

And I drew a bit apart,
    And I lagged a bit behind,
And I thought on Peace Eternal,
    Lest He look into my mind;

And I gazed upon the sky,
    And I thought of Heavenly Rest,—
And I slipped away like water
    Through the fingers of the blest!

All their eyes were fixed on Glory,
    Not a glance brushed over me;

"Alleluia! Alleluia!"
  Up the road,—and I was free.

And my heart rose like a freshet,
  And it swept me on before,
Giddy as a whirling stick,
  Till I felt the earth once more.

All the Earth was charred and black,
  Fire had swept from pole to pole;
And the bottom of the sea
  Was as brittle as a bowl;

And the timbered mountain-top
  Was as naked as a skull,—
Nothing left, nothing left,
  Of the Earth so beautiful!

"Earth," I said, "how can I leave you?"
  "You are all I have," I said;
"What is left to take my mind up,
  Living always, and you dead?"

"Speak!" I said, "Oh, tell me something!
  Make a sign that I can see!
For a keepsake! To keep always!
  Quick!—before God misses me!"

And I listened for a voice;—
  But my heart was all I heard;
Not a screech-owl, not a loon,
  Not a tree-toad said a word.

And I waited for a sign;—
  Coals and cinders, nothing more;
And a little cloud of smoke
  Floating on a valley floor.

And I peered into the smoke
  Till it rotted, like a fog:—
There, encompassed round by fire,
  Stood a blue-flag in a bog!

Little flames came wading out,
  Straining, straining towards its stem,

But it was so blue and tall
  That it scorned to think of them!

Red and thirsty were their tongues,
  As the tongues of wolves must be,
But it was so blue and tall—
  Oh, I laughed, I cried, to see!

All my heart became a tear,
  All my soul became a tower,
Never loved I anything
  As I loved that tall blue flower!

It was all the little boats
  That had ever sailed the sea,
It was all the little books
  That had gone to school with me;

On its roots like iron claws
  Rearing up so blue and tall,—
It was all the gallant Earth
  With its back against a wall!

In a breath, ere I had breathed,—
  Oh, I laughed, I cried, to see!—
I was kneeling at its side,
  And it leaned its head on me!

Crumbling stones and sliding sand
  Is the road to Heaven now;
Icy at my straining knees
  Drags the awful under-tow;

Soon but stepping-stones of dust
  Will the road to Heaven be,—
Father, Son and Holy Ghost,
  Reach a hand and rescue me!

"There—there, my blue-flag flower;
  Hush—hush—go to sleep;
That is only God you hear,
  Counting up His folded sheep!

Lullabye—lullabye—
  That is only God that calls,

Missing me, seeking me,
   Ere the road to nothing falls!

He will set His mighty feet
   Firmly on the sliding sand;
Like a little frightened bird
   I will creep into His hand;

I will tell Him all my grief,
   I will tell Him all my sin;
He will give me half His robe
   For a cloak to wrap you in.

Lullabye—lullabye—"
   Rocks the burnt-out planet free!—
Father, Son and Holy Ghost,
   Reach a hand and rescue me!

Ah, the voice of love at last!
   Lo, at last the face of light!
And the whole of His white robe
   For a cloak against the night!

And upon my heart asleep
   All the things I ever knew!—
"Holds Heaven not some cranny, Lord,
   For a flower so tall and blue?"

All's well and all's well!
   Gay the lights of Heaven show!
In some moist and Heavenly place
   We will set it out to grow.

Journey

Ah, could I lay me down in this long grass
And close my eyes, and let the quiet wind
Blow over me,—I am so tired, so tired
Of passing pleasant places! All my life,
Following Care along the dusty road,
Have I looked back at loveliness and sighed;
Yet at my hand an unrelenting hand
Tugged ever, and I passed. All my life long

Over my shoulder have I looked at peace;
And now I fain would lie in this long grass
And close my eyes.
                    Yet onward!
                              Cat-birds call
Through the long afternoon, and creeks at dusk
Are guttural. Whip-poor-wills wake and cry,
Drawing the twilight close about their throats.
Only my heart makes answer. Eager vines
Go up the rocks and wait; flushed apple-trees
Pause in their dance and break the ring for me;
Dim, shady wood-roads, redolent of fern
And bayberry, that through sweet bevies thread
Of round-faced roses, pink and petulant,
Look back and beckon ere they disappear.
Only my heart, only my heart responds.
Yet, ah, my path is sweet on either side
All through the dragging day,—sharp underfoot,
And hot, and like dead mist the dry dust hangs—
But far, oh, far as passionate eye can reach,
And long, ah, long as rapturous eye can cling,
The world is mine: blue hill, still silver lake,
Broad field, bright flower, and the long white road.
A gateless garden, and an open path:
My feet to follow, and my heart to hold.

Eel-Grass

No matter what I say,
    All that I really love
Is the rain that flattens on the bay,
    And the eel-grass in the cove;
The jingle-shells that lie and bleach
    At the tide-line, and the trace
Of higher tides along the beach:
    Nothing in this place.

Elegy Before Death

There will be rose and rhododendron
    When you are dead and under ground;

Still will be heard from white syringas
    Heavy with bees, a sunny sound;

Still will the tamaracks be raining
    After the rain has ceased, and still
Will there be robins in the stubble,
    Brown sheep upon the warm green hill.

Spring will not ail nor autumn falter;
    Nothing will know that you are gone,
Saving alone some sullen plough-land
    None but yourself sets foot upon;

Saving the may-weed and the pig-weed
    Nothing will know that you are dead,—
These, and perhaps a useless wagon
    Standing beside some tumbled shed.

Oh, there will pass with your great passing
    Little of beauty not your own,—
Only the light from common water,
    Only the grace from simple stone!

The Bean-Stalk

Ho, Giant! This is I!
I have built me a bean-stalk into your sky!
La,—but it's lovely, up so high!

This is how I came,—I put
Here my knee, there my foot,
Up and up, from shoot to shoot—
And the blessèd bean-stalk thinning
Like the mischief all the time,
Till it took me rocking, spinning,
In a dizzy, sunny circle,
Making angles with the root,
Far and out above the cackle
Of the city I was born in,
Till the little dirty city
In the light so sheer and sunny
Shone as dazzling bright and pretty
As the money that you find

In a dream of finding money—
What a wind! What a morning!—

Till the tiny, shiny city,
When I shot a glance below,
Shaken with a giddy laughter,
Sick and blissfully afraid,
Was a dew-drop on a blade,
And a pair of moments after
Was the whirling guess I made,—
And the wind was like a whip
Cracking past my icy ears,
And my hair stood out behind,
And my eyes were full of tears,
Wide-open and cold,
More tears than they could hold,
The wind was blowing so,
And my teeth were in a row,
Dry and grinning,
And I felt my foot slip,
And I scratched the wind and whined,
And I clutched the stalk and jabbered,
With my eyes shut blind,—
What a wind! What a wind!

Your broad sky, Giant,
Is the shelf of a cupboard;
I make bean-stalks, I'm
A builder, like yourself,
But bean-stalks is my trade,
I couldn't make a shelf,
Don't know how they're made,
Now, a bean-stalk is more pliant—
La, what a climb!

Weeds

White with daisies and red with sorrel
    And empty, empty under the sky!—
Life is a quest and love a quarrel—
    Here is a place for me to lie.

Daisies spring from damnèd seeds,
　　And this red fire that here I see
Is a worthless crop of crimson weeds,
　　Cursed by farmers thriftily.

But here, unhated for an hour,
　　The sorrel runs in ragged flame,
The daisy stands, a bastard flower,
　　Like flowers that bear an honest name.

And here a while, where no wind brings
　　The baying of a pack athirst,
May sleep the sleep of blessèd things
　　The blood too bright, the brow accurst.

Passer Mortuus Est

Death devours all lovely things;
　　Lesbia with her sparrow
Shares the darkness,—presently
　　Every bed is narrow

Unremembered as old rain
　　Dries the sheer libation,
And the little petulant hand
　　Is an annotation.

After all, my erstwhile dear,
　　My no longer cherished,
Need we say it was not love,
　　Now that love is perished?

Pastoral

If it were only still!—
With far away the shrill
Crying of a cock;
Or the shaken bell
From a cow's throat
Moving through the bushes;
Or the soft shock
Of wizened apples falling
From an old tree

In a forgotten orchard
Upon the hilly rock!

Oh, grey hill,
Where the grazing herd
Licks the purple blossom,
Crops the spiky weed!
Oh, stony pasture,
Where the tall mullein
Stands up so sturdy
On its little seed!

Assault

I

I had forgotten how the frogs must sound
After a year of silence, else I think
I should not so have ventured forth alone
At dusk upon this unfrequented road.

II

I am waylaid by Beauty. Who will walk
Between me and the crying of the frogs?
Oh, savage Beauty, suffer me to pass,
That am a timid woman, on her way
From one house to another!

Travel

The railroad track is miles away,
    And the day is loud with voices speaking,
Yet there isn't a train goes by all day
    But I hear its whistle shrieking.

All night there isn't a train goes by,
    Though the night is still for sleep and dreaming
But I see its cinders red on the sky,
    And hear its engine steaming.

My heart is warm with the friends I make,
    And better friends I'll not be knowing,
Yet there isn't a train I wouldn't take,
    No matter where it's going.

Low-Tide

These wet rocks where the tide has been,
  Barnacled white and weeded brown
And slimed beneath to a beautiful green,
  These wet rocks where the tide went down
Will show again when the tide is high
  Faint and perilous, far from shore,
No place to dream, but a place to die,—
  The bottom of the sea once more.
There was a child that wandered through
  A giant's empty house all day,—
House full of wonderful things and new,
  But no fit place for a child to play.

Song of a Second April

April this year, not otherwise
  Than April of a year ago,
Is full of whispers, full of sighs,
  Of dazzling mud and dingy snow;
  Hepaticas that pleased you so
Are here again, and butterflies.

There rings a hammering all day,
  And shingles lie about the doors;
In orchards near and far away
  The grey wood-pecker taps and bores;
  And men are merry at their chores,
And children earnest at their play.

The larger streams run still and deep,
  Noisy and swift the small brooks run
Among the mullein stalks the sheep
  Go up the hillside in the sun,
  Pensively,—only you are gone,
You that alone I cared to keep.

Rosemary

For the sake of some things
  That be now no more

I will strew rushes
   On my chamber-floor,
I will plant bergamot
   At my kitchen-door.

For the sake of dim things
   That were once so plain
I will set a barrel
   Out to catch the rain,
I will hang an iron pot
   On an iron crane.

Many things be dead and gone
   That were brave and gay;
For the sake of these things
   I will learn to say,
"An it please you, gentle sirs,"
   "Alack!" and "Well-a-day!"

The Poet and His Book

Down, you mongrel, Death!
   Back into your kennel!
I have stolen breath
   In a stalk of fennel!
You shall scratch and you shall whine
   Many a night, and you shall worry
   Many a bone, before you bury
One sweet bone of mine!

When shall I be dead?
   When my flesh is withered,
And above my head
   Yellow pollen gathered
All the empty afternoon?
   When sweet lovers pause and wonder
   Who am I that lie thereunder,
Hidden from the moon?

This my personal death?—
   That my lungs be failing
To inhale the breath
   Others are exhaling?

This my subtle spirit's end?—
    Ah, when the thawed winter splashes
    Over these chance dust and ashes,
Weep not me, my friend!

Me, by no means dead
    In that hour, but surely
When this book, unread,
    Rots to earth obscurely,
And no more to any breast,
    Close against the clamorous swelling
    Of the thing there is no telling,
Are these pages pressed!

When this book is mould,
    And a book of many
Waiting to be sold
    For a casual penny,
In a little open case,
    In a street unclean and cluttered,
    Where a heavy mud is spattered
From the passing drays,

Stranger, pause and look;
    From the dust of ages
Lift this little book,
    Turn the tattered pages,
Read me, do not let me die!
    Search the fading letters, finding
    Steadfast in the broken binding
All that once was I!

When these veins are weeds,
    When these hollowed sockets
Watch the rooty seeds
    Bursting down like rockets,
And surmise the spring again,
    Or, remote in that black cupboard,
    Watch the pink worms writhing upward
At the smell of rain,

Boys and girls that lie
    Whispering in the hedges,
Do not let me die,
    Mix me with your pledges;

Boys and girls that slowly walk
    In the woods, and weep, and quarrel,
    Staring past the pink wild laurel,
Mix me with your talk,

Do not let me die!
    Farmers at your raking,
When the sun is high,
    While the hay is making,
When, along the stubble strewn,
    Withering on their stalks uneaten,
    Strawberries turn dark and sweeten
In the lapse of noon;

Shepherds on the hills,
    In the pastures, drowsing
To the tinkling bells
    Of the brown sheep browsing;
Sailors crying through the storm;
    Scholars at your study; hunters
    Lost amid the whirling winter's
Whiteness uniform;

Men that long for sleep;
    Men that wake and revel;—
If an old song leap
    To your senses' level
At such moments, may it be
    Sometimes, though a moment only,
    Some forgotten, quaint and homely
Vehicle of me!

Women at your toil,
    Women at your leisure
Till the kettle boil,
    Snatch of me your pleasure,
Where the broom-straw marks the leaf;
    Women quiet with your weeping
    Lest you wake a workman sleeping,
Mix me with your grief!

Boys and girls that steal
    From the shocking laughter
Of the old, to kneel
    By a dripping rafter

Under the discolored eaves,
   Out of trunks with hingeless covers
   Lifting tales of saints and lovers,
Travelers, goblins, thieves,

Suns that shine by night,
   Mountains made from valleys,—
Bear me to the light,
   Flat upon your bellies
By the webby window lie,
   Where the little flies are crawling,—
   Read me, margin me with scrawling,
Do not let me die!

Sexton, ply your trade!
   In a shower of gravel
Stamp upon your spade!
   Many a rose shall ravel,
Many a metal wreath shall rust
   In the rain, and I go singing
   Through the lots where you are flinging
Yellow clay on dust!

Alms

My heart is what it was before,
   A house where people come and go;
But it is winter with your love,—
   The sashes are beset with snow.

I light the lamp and lay the cloth
   I blow the coals to blaze again;
But it is winter with your love,
   The frost is thick upon the pane.

I know a winter when it comes:
   The leaves are listless on the boughs;
I watched your love a little while,
   And brought my plants into the house.

I water them and turn them south,
   I snap the dead brown from the stem;
But it is winter with your love,—
   I only tend and water them.

There was a time I stood and watched
   The small, ill-natured sparrows' fray;
I loved the beggar that I fed,
   I cared for what he had to say,

I stood and watched him out of sight;
   Today I reach around the door
And set a bowl upon the step;
   My heart is what it was before,

But it is winter with your love;
   I scatter crumbs upon the sill,
And close the window,—and the birds
   May take or leave them, as they will.

Inland

People that build their houses inland,
   People that buy a plot of ground
Shaped like a house, and build a house there,
   Far from the sea-board, far from the sound

Of water sucking the hollow ledges,
   Tons of water striking the shore,—
What do they long for, as I long for
   One salt smell of the sea once more?

People the waves have not awakened,
   Spanking the boats at the harbor's head,
What do they long for, as I long for,—
   Starting up in my inland bed,

Beating the narrow walls, and finding
   Neither a window nor a door,
Screaming to God for death by drowning,—
   One salt taste of the sea once more?

To a Poet That Died Young

Minstrel, what have you to do
With this man that, after you,
Sharing not your happy fate,
Sat as England's Laureate?

Vainly, in these iron days,
Strives the poet in your praise,
Minstrel, by whose singing side
Beauty walked, until you died.

Still, though none should hark again,
Drones the blue-fly in the pane,
Thickly crusts the blackest moss,
Blows the rose its musk across,
Floats the boat that is forgot
None the less to Camelot.

Many a bard's untimely death
Lends unto his verses breath;
Here's a song was never sung:
Growing old is dying young.
Minstrel, what is this to you:
That a man you never knew,
When your grave was far and green,
Sat and gossipped with a queen?

Thalia knows how rare a thing
Is it, to grow old and sing;
When a brown and tepid tide
Closes in on every side.
Who shall say if Shelley's gold
Had withstood it to grow old?

Wraith

"Thin Rain, whom are you haunting,
 That you haunt my door?"
—Surely it is not I she's wanting;
 Someone living here before—
"Nobody's in the house but me:
You may come in if you like and see."

Thin as thread, with exquisite fingers,—
 Have you seen her, any of you?—
Grey shawl, and leaning on the wind,
 And the garden showing through?

Glimmering eyes,—and silent, mostly,
 Sort of a whisper, sort of a purr,

Asking something, asking it over,
   If you get a sound from her.—

Ever see her, any of you?—
   Strangest thing I've ever known,—
Every night since I moved in,
   And I came to be alone.

"Thin Rain, hush with your knocking!
   You may not come in!
This is I that you hear rocking;
   Nobody's with me, nor has been!"

Curious, how she tried the window,—
   Odd, the way she tries the door,—
Wonder just what sort of people
   Could have had this house before . . .

Ebb

I know what my heart is like
   Since your love died:
It is like a hollow ledge
Holding a little pool
   Left there by the tide,
   A little tepid pool,
Drying inward from the edge.

Elaine

Oh, come again to Astolat!
   I will not ask you to be kind.
And you may go when you will go,
   And I will stay behind.

I will not say how dear you are,
   Or ask you if you hold me dear,
Or trouble you with things for you
   The way I did last year.

So still the orchard, Lancelot,
   So very still the lake shall be,

You could not guess—though you should guess—
  What is become of me.

So wide shall be the garden-walk,
  The garden-seat so very wide,
You needs must think—if you should think—
  The lily maid had died.

Save that, a little way away,
  I'd watch you for a little while,
To see you speak, the way you speak,
  And smile,—if you should smile.

Burial

Mine is a body that should die at sea!
  And have for a grave, instead of a grave
Six feet deep and the length of me,
  All the water that is under the wave!

And terrible fishes to seize my flesh,
  Such as a living man might fear,
And eat me while I am firm and fresh,—
  Not wait till I've been dead for a year!

Mariposa

Butterflies are white and blue
In this field we wander through.
Suffer me to take your hand.
Death comes in a day or two.

All the things we ever knew
Will be ashes in that hour,
Mark the transient butterfly,
How he hangs upon the flower.

Suffer me to take your hand.
Suffer me to cherish you
Till the dawn is in the sky.
Whether I be false or true,
Death comes in a day or two.

The Little Hill

Oh, here the air is sweet and still,
    And soft's the grass to lie on;
And far away's the little hill
    They took for Christ to die on.

And there's a hill across the brook,
    And down the brook's another;
But, oh, the little hill they took,—
    I think I am its mother!

The moon that saw Gethsemane,
    I watch it rise and set;
It has so many things to see,
    They help it to forget.

But little hills that sit at home
    So many hundred years,
Remember Greece, remember Rome,
    Remember Mary's tears.

And far away in Palestine,
    Sadder than any other,
Grieves still the hill that I call mine,—
    I think I am its mother!

Doubt No More That Oberon

Doubt no more that Oberon—
Never doubt that Pan
Lived, and played a reed, and ran
After nymphs in a dark forest,
In the merry, credulous days,—
Lived, and led a fairy band
Over the indulgent land!
Ah, for in this dourest, sorest
Age man's eye has looked upon,
Death to fauns and death to fays,
Still the dog-wood dares to raise—
Healthy tree, with trunk and root--
Ivory bowls that bear no fruit,

And the starlings and the jays—
Birds that cannot even sing—
Dare to come again in spring!

Lament

Listen, children:
Your father is dead.
From his old coats
I'll make you little jackets;
I'll make you little trousers
From his old pants.
There'll be in his pockets
Things he used to put there,
Keys and pennies
Covered with tobacco;
Dan shall have the pennies
To save in his bank;
Anne shall have the keys
To make a pretty noise with.
Life must go on,
And the dead be forgotten;
Life must go on,
Though good men die;
Anne, eat your breakfast;
Dan, take your medicine;
Life must go on;
I forget just why.

Exiled

Searching my heart for its true sorrow,
 This is the thing I find to be:
That I am weary of words and people,
 Sick of the city, wanting the sea;

Wanting the sticky, salty sweetness
 Of the strong wind and shattered spray;
Wanting the loud sound and the soft sound
 Of the big surf that breaks all day.

Always before about my dooryard,
    Marking the reach of the winter sea,
Rooted in sand and dragging drift-wood,
    Straggled the purple wild sweet-pea;

Always I climbed the wave at morning,
    Shook the sand from my shoes at night,
That now am caught beneath great buildings,
    Stricken with noise, confused with light.

If I could hear the green piles groaning
    Under the windy wooden piers,
See once again the bobbing barrels,
    And the black sticks that fence the weirs,

If I could see the weedy mussels
    Crusting the wrecked and rotting hulls,
Hear once again the hungry crying
    Overhead, of the wheeling gulls,

Feel once again the shanty straining
    Under the turning of the tide,
Fear once again the rising freshet,
    Dread the bell in the fog outside, —

I should be happy, — that was happy
    All day long on the coast of Maine!
I have a need to hold and handle
    Shells and anchors and ships again!

I should be happy, that am happy
    Never at all since I came here.
I am too long away from water.
    I have a need of water near.

The Death of Autumn

When reeds are dead and a straw to thatch the marshes,
And feathered pampas-grass rides into the wind
Like agèd warriors westward, tragic, thinned
Of half their tribe, and over the flattened rushes,
Stripped of its secret, open, stark and bleak,
Blackens afar the half-forgotten creek, —

Then leans on me the weight of the year, and crushes
My heart. I know that Beauty must ail and die,
And will be born again,—but ah, to see
Beauty stiffened, staring up at the sky!
Oh, Autumn! Autumn!—What is the Spring to me?

Ode to Silence

Aye, but she?
Your other sister and my other soul
Grave Silence, lovelier
Than the three loveliest maidens, what of her?
Clio, not you,
Not you, Calliope,
Nor all your wanton line,
Not Beauty's perfect self shall comfort me
For Silence once departed,
For her the cool-tongued, her the tranquil-hearted,
Whom evermore I follow wistfully,
Wandering Heaven and Earth and Hell and the four seasons through;
Thalia, not you,
Not you, Melpomene,
Not your incomparable feet, O thin Terpsichore,
I seek in this great hall,
But one more pale, more pensive, most beloved of you all.

I seek her from afar.
I come from temples where her altars are,
From groves that bear her name,
Noisy with stricken victims now and sacrificial flame,
And cymbals struck on high and strident faces
Obstreperous in her praise
They neither love nor know,
A goddess of gone days,
Departed long ago,
Abandoning the invaded shrines and fanes
Of her old sanctuary,
A deity obscure and legendary,
Of whom there now remains,
For sages to decipher and priests to garble,
Only and for a little while her letters wedged in marble,
Which even now, behold, the friendly mumbling rain erases,

And the inarticulate snow,
Leaving at last of her least signs and traces
None whatsoever, nor whither she is vanished from these places.

"She will love well," I said,
"If love be of that heart inhabiter,
The flowers of the dead;
The red anemone that with no sound
Moves in the wind, and from another wound
That sprang, the heavily-sweet blue hyacinth,
That blossoms underground,
And sallow poppies, will be dear to her.
And will not Silence know
In the black shade of what obsidian steep
Stiffens the white narcissus numb with sleep?
(Seed which Demeter's daughter bore from home,
Uptorn by desperate fingers long ago,
Reluctant even as she,
Undone Persephone,
And even as she set out again to grow
In twilight, in perdition's lean and inauspicious loam).
She will love well," I said,
"The flowers of the dead;
Where dark Persephone the winter round,
Uncomforted for home, uncomforted,
Lacking a sunny southern slope in northern Sicily,
With sullen pupils focussed on a dream,
Stares on the stagnant stream
That moats the unequivocable battlements of Hell,
There, there will she be found,
She that is Beauty veiled from men and Music in a swound."

"I long for Silence as they long for breath
Whose helpless nostrils drink the bitter sea;
What thing can be
So stout, what so redoubtable, in Death
What fury, what considerable rage, if only she,
Upon whose icy breast,
Unquestioned, uncaressed,
One time I lay,
And whom always I lack,
Even to this day,
Being by no means from that frigid bosom weaned away,
If only she therewith be given me back?"

I sought her down that dolorous labyrinth,
Wherein no shaft of sunlight ever fell,
And in among the bloodless everywhere
I sought her, but the air,
Breathed many times and spent,
Was fretful with a whispering discontent,
And questioning me, importuning me to tell
Some slightest tidings of the light of day they know no more,
Plucking my sleeve, the eager shades were with me where I went.
I paused at every grievous door,
And harked a moment, holding up my hand,—and for a space
A hush was on them, while they watched my face;
And then they fell a-whispering as before;
So that I smiled at them and left them, seeing she was not there.

I sought her, too,
Among the upper gods, although I knew
She was not like to be where feasting is,
Nor near to Heaven's lord,
Being a thing abhorred
And shunned of him, although a child of his,
(Not yours, not yours; to you she owes not breath,
Mother of Song, being sown of Zeus upon a dream of Death).
Fearing to pass unvisited some place
And later learn, too late, how all the while,
With her still face,
She had been standing there and seen me pass, without a smile,
I sought her even to the sagging board whereat
The stout immortals sat;
But such a laughter shook the mighty hall
No one could hear me say:
Had she been seen upon the Hill that day?
And no one knew at all
How long I stood, or when at last I sighed and went away.

There is a garden lying in a lull
Between the mountains and the mountainous sea,
I know not where, but which a dream diurnal
Paints on my lids a moment till the hull
Be lifted from the kernel
And Slumber fed to me.
Your foot-print is not there, Mnemosene,
Though it would seem a ruined place and after
Your lichenous heart, being full

Of broken columns, caryatides
Thrown to the earth and fallen forward on their jointless knees,
And urns funereal altered into dust
Minuter than the ashes of the dead,
And Psyche's lamp out of the earth up-thrust,
Dripping itself in marble wax on what was once the bed
Of Love, and his young body asleep, but now is dust instead.

There twists the bitter-sweet, the white wisteria
Fastens its fingers in the strangling wall,
And the wide crannies quicken with bright weeds;
There dumbly like a worm all day the still white orchid feeds;
But never an echo of your daughters' laughter
Is there, nor any sign of you at all
Swells fungous from the rotten bough, grey mother of Pieria!

Only her shadow once upon a stone
I saw,—and, lo, the shadow and the garden, too, were gone.

I tell you you have done her body an ill,
You chatterers, you noisy crew!
She is not anywhere!
I sought her in deep Hell;
And through the world as well;
I thought of Heaven and I sought her there;
Above nor under ground
Is Silence to be found,
That was the very warp and woof of you,
Lovely before your songs began and after they were through!
Oh, say if on this hill
Somewhere your sister's body lies in death,
So I may follow there, and make a wreath
Of my locked hands, that on her quiet breast
Shall lie till age has withered them!

                    (Ah, sweetly from the rest
I see
Turn and consider me
Compassionate Euterpe!)
"There is a gate beyond the gate of Death,
Beyond the gate of everlasting Life,
Beyond the gates of Heaven and Hell," she saith,
"Whereon but to believe is horror!
Whereon to meditate engendereth
Even in deathless spirits such as I

A tumult in the breath,
A chilling of the inexhaustible blood
Even in my veins that never will be dry,
And in the austere, divine monotony
That is my being, the madness of an unaccustomed mood.

This is her province whom you lack and seek;
And seek her not elsewhere.
Hell is a thoroughfare
For pilgrims,—Herakles,
And he that loved Euridice too well,
Have walked therein; and many more than these;
And witnessed the desire and the despair
Of souls that passed reluctantly and sicken for the air;
You, too, have entered Hell,
And issued thence; but thence whereof I speak
None has returned;—for thither fury brings
Only the driven ghosts of them that flee before all things.
Oblivion is the name of this abode: and she is there."

Oh, radiant Song! Oh, gracious Memory!
Be long upon this height
I shall not climb again!
I know the way you mean,—the little night,
And the long empty day,—never to see
Again the angry light,
Or hear the hungry noises cry my brain!

Ah, but she,
Your other sister and my other soul,
She shall again be mine;
And I shall drink her from a silver bowl,
A chilly thin green wine,
Not bitter to the taste,
Not sweet,
Not of your press, oh, restless, clamorous nine,—
To foam beneath the frantic hoofs of mirth—
But savoring faintly of the acid earth,
And trod by pensive feet
From perfect clusters ripened without haste
Out of the urgent heat
In some clear glimmering vaulted twilight under the odorous vine.

Lift up your lyres! Sing on!
But as for me, I seek your sister whither she is gone.

MEMORIAL TO D. C.*

[VASSAR COLLEGE, 1918]

Oh, loveliest throat of all sweet throats,
Where now no more the music is,
With hands that wrote you little notes
I write you little elegies!

Epitaph

Heap not on this mound
   Roses that she loved so well;
Why bewilder her with roses,
   That she cannot see or smell?
She is happy where she lies
With the dust upon her eyes.

Prayer to Persephone

Be to her, Persephone,
All the things I might not be;
Take her head upon your knee.
She that was so proud and wild,
Flippant, arrogant and free,
She that had no need of me,
Is a little lonely child
Lost in Hell,—Persephone,
Take her head upon your knee;
Say to her, "My dear, my dear,
It is not so dreadful here."

Chorus

Give away her gowns,
Give away her shoes;
She has no more use
For her fragrant gowns;

---

*Includes the following six poems.

Take them all down,
Blue, green, blue,
Lilac, pink, blue,
From their padded hangers;
She will dance no more
In her narrow shoes;
Sweep her narrow shoes
From the closet floor.

Elegy

Let them bury your big eyes
In the secret earth securely,
Your thin fingers, and your fair,
Soft, indefinite-colored hair,—
All of these in some way, surely,
From the secret earth shall rise;
Not for these I sit and stare,
Broken and bereft completely;
Your young flesh that sat so neatly
On your little bones will sweetly
Blossom in the air.

But your voice,—never the rushing
Of a river underground,
Not the rising of the wind
In the trees before the rain,
Not the woodcock's watery call,
Not the note the white-throat utters,
Not the feet of children pushing
Yellow leaves along the gutters
In the blue and bitter fall,
Shall content my musing mind
For the beauty of that sound
That in no new way at all
Ever will be heard again.

Sweetly through the sappy stalk
Of the vigorous weed,
Holding all it held before,
Cherished by the faithful sun,
On and on eternally
Shall your altered fluid run,

Bud and bloom and go to seed;
But your singing days are done;
But the music of your talk
Never shall the chemistry
Of the secret earth restore.
All your lovely words are spoken.
Once the ivory box is broken,
Beats the golden bird no more.

Dirge

Boys and girls that held her dear,
   Do your weeping now;
All you loved of her lies here.

Brought to earth the arrogant brow,
   And the withering tongue
Chastened; do your weeping now.

Sing whatever songs are sung,
   Wind whatever wreath,
For a playmate perished young,

For a spirit spent in death.
Boys and girls that held her dear,
All you loved of her lies here.

TWELVE SONNETS

I

We talk of taxes, and I call you friend;
Well, such you are,—but well enough we know
How thick about us root, how rankly grow
Those subtle weeds no man has need to tend,
That flourish through neglect, and soon must send
Perfume too sweet upon us and overthrow
Our steady senses; how such matters go
We are aware, and how such matters end.
Yet shall be told no meagre passion here;
With lovers such as we forevermore
Isolde drinks the draught, and Guinevere
Receives the Table's ruin through her door,

Francesca, with the loud surf at her ear,
Lets fall the colored book upon the floor.

II

Into the golden vessel of great song
Let us pour all our passion; breast to breast
Let other lovers lie, in love and rest;
Not we,—articulate, so, but with the tongue
Of all the world: the churning blood, the long
Shuddering quiet, the desperate hot palms pressed
Sharply together upon the escaping guest,
The common soul, unguarded, and grown strong.
Longing alone is singer to the lute;
Let still on nettles in the open sigh
The minstrel, that in slumber is as mute
As any man, and love be far and high,
That else forsakes the topmost branch, a fruit
Found on the ground by every passer-by.

III

Not with libations, but with shouts and laughter
We drenched the altars of Love's sacred grove,
Shaking to earth green fruits, impatient after
The launching of the colored moths of Love.
Love's proper myrtle and his mother's zone
We bound about our irreligious brows,
And fettered him with garlands of our own,
And spread a banquet in his frugal house.
Not yet the god has spoken; but I fear
Though we should break our bodies in his flame,
And pour our blood upon his altar, here
Henceforward is a grove without a name,
A pasture to the shaggy goats of Pan,
Whence flee forever a woman and a man.

IV

Only until this cigarette is ended,
A little moment at the end of all,

While on the floor the quiet ashes fall,
And in the firelight to a lance extended,
Bizarrely with the jazzing music blended,
The broken shadow dances on the wall,
I will permit my memory to recall
The vision of you, by all my dreams attended.
And then adieu,—farewell!—the dream is done.
Yours is a face of which I can forget
The color and the features, every one,
The words not ever, and the smiles not yet;
But in your day this moment is the sun
Upon a hill, after the sun has set.

V

Once more into my arid days like dew,
Like wind from on oasis, or the sound
Of cold sweet water bubbling underground,
A treacherous messenger, the thought of you
Comes to destroy me; once more I renew
Firm faith in your abundance, whom I found
Long since to be but just one other mound
Of sand, whereon no green thing ever grew.
And once again, and wiser in no wise,
I chase your colored phantom on the air,
And sob and curse and fall and weep and rise
And stumble pitifully on to where,
Miserable and lost, with stinging eyes,
Once more I clasp,—and there is nothing there.

VI

No rose that in a garden ever grew,
In Homer's or in Omar's or in mine,
Though buried under centuries of fine
Dead dust of roses, shut from sun and dew
Forever, and forever lost from view,
But must again in fragrance rich as wine
The grey aisles of the air incarnadine
When the old summers surge into a new.

Thus when I swear, "I love with all my heart,"
'Tis with the heart of Lilith that I swear,
'Tis with the love of Lesbia and Lucrece;
And thus as well my love must lose some part
Of what it is, had Helen been less fair,
Or perished young, or stayed at home in Greece.

VII

When I too long have looked upon your face,
Wherein for me a brightness unobscured
Save by the mists of brightness has its place,
And terrible beauty not to be endured,
I turn away reluctant from your light,
And stand irresolute, a mind undone,
A silly, dazzled thing deprived of sight
From having looked too long upon the sun.
Then is my daily life a narrow room
In which a little while, uncertainly,
Surrounded by impenetrable gloom,
Among familiar things grown strange to me
Making my way, I pause, and feel, and hark,
Till I become accustomed to the dark.

VIII

And you as well must die, belovèd dust,
And all your beauty stand you in no stead;
This flawless, vital hand, this perfect head,
This body of flame and steel, before the gust
Of Death, or under his autumnal frost,
Shall be as any leaf, be no less dead
Than the first leaf that fell,—this wonder fled.
Altered, estranged, disintegrated, lost.
Nor shall my love avail you in your hour.
In spite of all my love, you will arise
Upon that day and wander down the air
Obscurely as the unattended flower,
It mattering not how beautiful you were,
Or how belovèd above all else that dies.

IX

Let you not say of me when I am old,
In pretty worship of my withered hands
Forgetting who I am, and how the sands
Of such a life as mine run red and gold
Even to the ultimate sifting dust, "Behold,
Here walketh passionless age!"—for there expands
A curious superstition in these lands,
And by its leave some weightless tales are told.

In me no lenten wicks watch out the night;
I am the booth where Folly holds her fair;
Impious no less in ruin than in strength,
When I lie crumbled to the earth at length,
Let you not say, "Upon this reverend site
The righteous groaned and beat their breasts in prayer."

X

Oh, my belovèd, have you thought of this:
How in the years to come unscrupulous Time,
More cruel than Death, will tear you from my kiss,
And make you old, and leave me in my prime?
How you and I, who scale together yet
A little while the sweet, immortal height
No pilgrim may remember or forget,
As sure as the world turns, some granite night
Shall lie awake and know the gracious flame
Gone out forever on the mutual stone;
And call to mind that on the day you came
I was a child, and you a hero grown?—
And the night pass, and the strange morning break
Upon our anguish for each other's sake!

XI

As to some lovely temple, tenantless
Long since, that once was sweet with shivering brass,
Knowing well its altars ruined and the grass
Grown up between the stones, yet from excess

Of grief hard driven, or great loneliness,
The worshiper returns, and those who pass
Marvel him crying on a name that was,—
So is it now with me in my distress.
Your body was a temple to Delight;
Cold are its ashes whence the breath is fled,
Yet here one time your spirit was wont to move;
Here might I hope to find you day or night,
And here I come to look for you, my love,
Even now, foolishly, knowing you are dead.

XII

Cherish you then the hope I shall forget
At length, my lord, Pieria?—put away
For your so passing sake, this mouth of clay,
These mortal bones against my body set,
For all the puny fever and frail sweat
Of human love,—renounce for these, I say,
The Singing Mountain's memory, and betray
The silent lyre that hangs upon me yet?
Ah, but indeed, some day shall you awake,
Rather, from dreams of me, that at your side
So many nights, a lover and a bride,
But stern in my soul's chastity, have lain,
To walk the world forever for my sake,
And in each chamber find me gone again!

Wild Swans

I looked in my heart while the wild swans went over.
And what did I see I had not seen before?
Only a question less or a question more;
Nothing to match the flight of wild birds flying.
Tiresome heart, forever living and dying,
House without air, I leave you and lock your door
Wild swans, come over the town, come over
The town again, trailing your legs and crying!

Index of First Lines